YOUR KNOWLEDGE HAS VALUE

- We will publish your bachelor's and master's thesis, essays and papers

- Your own eBook and book - sold worldwide in all relevant shops

- Earn money with each sale

Upload your text at www.GRIN.com
and publish for free

Bibliographic information published by the German National Library:

The German National Library lists this publication in the National Bibliography; detailed bibliographic data are available on the Internet at http://dnb.dnb.de .

This book is copyright material and must not be copied, reproduced, transferred, distributed, leased, licensed or publicly performed or used in any way except as specifically permitted in writing by the publishers, as allowed under the terms and conditions under which it was purchased or as strictly permitted by applicable copyright law. Any unauthorized distribution or use of this text may be a direct infringement of the author s and publisher s rights and those responsible may be liable in law accordingly.

Imprint:

Copyright © 2018 GRIN Verlag
Print and binding: Books on Demand GmbH, Norderstedt Germany
ISBN: 9783668700215

This book at GRIN:

https://www.grin.com/document/424846

Christina Haupt

Body Language.The Smile in Intercultural Communication

GRIN Verlag

GRIN - Your knowledge has value

Since its foundation in 1998, GRIN has specialized in publishing academic texts by students, college teachers and other academics as e-book and printed book. The website www.grin.com is an ideal platform for presenting term papers, final papers, scientific essays, dissertations and specialist books.

Visit us on the internet:

http://www.grin.com/

http://www.facebook.com/grincom

http://www.twitter.com/grin_com

Body Language:
The Smile in Intercultural Communication

Christina Haupt

Culture and Communication – Skills for Intercultural Communication

1. Introduction

"What is shown in the face is written there by culture." (as cited in Ekman and Keltner, 1997, p.28). This statement, which is attributed to Klineberg, gets to the heart of the discussion about facial body language in the intercultural context. Against the widespread belief that facial expressions are universally understood, I argue that smiling is a socially and culturally dependent phenomenon. The awareness of the perception and appropriateness of smiling in another society can be crucial to communicating successfully in an intercultural situation.

This paper first gives a theoretical overview of the topic, followed by a brief glimpse of the evolution of smiling. Then, attention is given to the exploration of smiling in different cultures. Furthermore, the connection between smiling, gender and power relations is displayed. Before concluding, the impact of lying on smiling is discussed.

During my research, Ekman and Keltner's essay (1997) was of great use. Among others, LaFrance and Hecht (1999) as well as Preuschoft and van Hooff (1997) gave fascinating insights into the topic.

2. Scientific Background

"Information which is overwhelming and too powerful cannot be conveyed by verbal means." (Ritchie Key, 1980, p.8). Such "overwhelming" information is usually connected to the experience of strong emotions. In the context of smiling, it is often naturally assumed that the display of a smile derives from a spontaneous reaction to a positive emotion, but this, in fact, is only a fraction of the truth (Weinberg and Konert, 1984; Pogosyan, 2017). Following the studies of Ekman, non-verbal communication consists of "illustrators" to support the spoken word, "emblems" which have a distinct culture-bound meaning, and "self-adaptors" in which someone's own body or clothes are being touched (Ekman and Keltner, 1997, p.30; Kendon, 1980, p.207; Harrison, 1987, p.323).

Moreover, he claims that there are nineteen different types of the human smile, which vary in form and meaning, i.e. enjoyment, affiliation, dominance, politeness or embarrassment (Ekman and Keltner, 1997, p.29; Krys 2016; LaFrance and Hecht, 1999, p.45). Smiles can roughly be distinguished into *false* and *real* (Ekman and Keltner, 1997, p.30; LaFrance and Hecht, 1999, p.46; Harrison, 1987, p.323). Based on studies of Duchenne in 1862, Ekman differentiates between "Non-Duchenne-Smiles" and "Duchenne-Smiles" (p.39). While both display "lip corner raising", only the latter involves the *orbicularis*-muscles (eye-muscles) and different brain areas, which indicates that the smile derives from an emotion (Ekman and Keltner, 1997, p.39f; LaFrance and Hecht, 1999, p.46; Harrison, 1987, p. 326; Lee and Wagner, 1999, p.283). The latter suggests that a speaker's non-verbal behaviour is related to his/her thoughts or words and thus always "self-synchronous" (Condon, 1980, p.53).

Occasionally, facial expressions do not match any of the above described if a "third field", e.g. eating, is involved (Ritchie Key, 1980, p.12).

3. The evolution of smiling

Non-verbal communication is deeply rooted in the evolution of human and non-human animals. Biologically, the brain develops patterns of movements in the earliest stage, the "reptilian brain", while the foundations of speech production are only created in the final, "new-mammalian", stage of an embryo's growth (Papousek and Papousek, 1997, p.93f.; Pogosyan 2017). Consequently, it is not surprising that gestures appear prior to the spoken word and come more naturally (Kendon, 1980, p.219, 227). Furthermore, ideas are automatically expressed verbally and non-verbally hence the same part of the human brain is responsible for speech production and movement (Ibid., p.208f.).

Human behaviour is best understood by looking at primates (particularly apes) that also use facial expressions to communicate with one another. The showing of "silent bared teeth", which resembles the human smile, is generally a sign of submission and consciously performed by the inferior animal or the superior in order to encourage the low-power partner. In contrast, joyful, spontaneous laughing with a "relaxed open mouth" is known as the "play face". This leads to the conclusion that smiling is not a universal sign of positive emotion, but rather a socially learned action (paragraph: Preuschoft and van Hooff, 1997, 172f., 183). The aspect of power relations is further discussed in point 5.

Although it is assumed that smiling is an innate action, for even embryos smile in the womb and blind babies smile when sleeping or hearing a human voice (Gutman 2011), there is strong evidence that smiling, to a large extent, is a product of culture. Segerstrale and Molnár call this the transition in which the "biological infant" becomes a "cultural being" (1997, p.10). Within the first hours, new-borns differentiate between familiar and unfamiliar and after a few weeks are able to imitate facial expressions (Goldschmidt, 1997, p.230). The mirroring of the mother's smile implies no emotional involvement, but rather is a sign of "affect hunger", which means that the infant learned that smiling evokes positive feedback in its culture (Ibid. p.232ff.).[1] Therefore, the "language of a cultural niche" is unconsciously and inevitably infiltrated into human beings from the very beginning (Papousek and Papousek, 1997, p.87).

Even as an adult, people automatically mirror facial expressions of others subconsciously, which leads to synchrony in groups (Segerstrale and Molnár, 1997, p.13f.; Ritchie Key, 1980, p.17). The innate mirroring of positive and negative expressions is called "Facial Feedback Hypothesis" and largely taken advantage of by the advertising industry ("Ten Ways", 2012). Thus, showing a smiling face in an advertisement unconsciously encourages the spectator to imitate the expression and, eventually, feel positive about the product.

4. Smiling in different cultures

Although body language is a universal cultural phenomenon, the cues to understanding it are not universal and are therefore culture-bound (Bernstein, 2017). Especially with the case of facial expressions such as smiling, it is culturally dependent whether smiles are expressed or masked

---

[1] This does not apply for every culture hence the smile of a child does not evoke positive feedback everywhere. See *4. Smiling in different cultures*.

(Weinberg and Konert, 1984). Therefore, it is inconsiderate of Motsumoto (as cited in Pogosyan, 2017) to assume that smiling is always a safe and positive sign in intercultural communication.

Keeping in mind that a mother's behaviour is "in accordance with local norms and cultural expectations" (Goldschmidt, 1997, p.241), the basis of the positive/negative connotation of smiling is laid at a very early stage in development. For instance, it is part of Sebei culture to maintain emotional detachment. Consequently, Sebei mothers rarely smile at their children (Ibid., p.237). Another rather extreme culture-bound example is the display of a smile in moments of loss, i.e. the death of a son in war, which women of Sparta and Samurai where expected to show (Ekman and Keltner, 1997, p.28).

The difficulty when talking about smiling is that for a long period of time most of the research has been conducted in so called "WEIRD"-societies (Western-Educated-Industrial-Rich-Democratic), which are not representative for the world (Krys, 2016; Petersen, 2016). Furthermore, it is important to keep in mind that even within a "WEIRD"-culture, there are personal differences among individuals, for even Darwin mentioned "the large class of idiots who are ... constantly smiling" negatively (as cited in Krys, 2016).

In "WEIRD" and low-context societies, smiling is generally perceived as a positive action (Bernstein, 2017). Therefore, it is of interest to focus on "Non-WEIRD" and high-context cultures in the following paragraphs, in which smiling often has a negative connotation.

Whereas in the USA it is considered polite and friendly to greet anyone with a smile (N.N., 2015), smiling at a stranger in Norway and Poland is seen as "insane" (Krys, 2016). In Russia, "smiling/laughing with no reason is a sign of stupidity" (Krys, 2016; Khazan, 2016). Therefore, Russians tend to maintain serious faces, even in photographs (Khazan, 2016).

According to Krys (2016), smiling is often closely linked to high uncertainty-avoidance. In contrast, "corruption corrupts" the naturally positive connotation of smiling hence it leads to scepticism towards a person's intelligence and trustworthiness. Her study showed the following results: Countries like Japan, Russia and France rated the intelligence of smiling people low, whereas participants from Germany, China and the UK rated it high. The honesty of a smiling person was denied in e.g. India, Argentina and Indonesia and reassured in Switzerland, Australia, and the Philippines. Consequently, the perception of a smile is not geographically or economically determined, but rather culturally.

In the previous research, much attention was given to the juxtaposition of the USA and Japan or China. A study conducted by Ekman and Keltner (1997, p.32) found out that US-Americans and Japanese displayed similar expressions when alone, but the Japanese expressed less negative emotions in the presence of another person. Moreover, it is deeply rooted in Japanese culture to "mask" negative feelings with smiles (Ramsey, 19834, p.141; Lee and Wagner, 1999, p.275). Therefore, Japanese display more non-Duchenne smiles in business interaction than US-Americans (LaFrance and Hecht, 1999, p.51; N.N., 2015). In Japanese culture, more attention is given to the expression of the eyes rather than the mouth, for the eyes cannot supress whether a smile is felt of faked (Ibid.).

In Chinese culture, "low-arousal positive states" (calm, harmony) are valued over "high-arousal positive states" (excitement). Therefore, small smiles with closed lips are performed more frequently than open smiles (Goldhill, 2016). Additionally, the way in which a leader performs a smile often gives clues about his/her culture (Ibid.).

Moving on to China's neighbouring country, India, it is worth noting that up until recent years, Indian brides were not supposed to smile during their wedding in order to display "female shyness" (N.N., 2015). However, with the continuous globalisation of the world, this tradition is slowly changing. Nowadays, 'non-smiling' cultures sometimes feel the need to adapt when interacting with 'smiling' ones (Ibid.). Furthermore, some collectivistic Eastern countries are also influenced by Western individualism, which can be seen in terms of advertisements (Diehl et al., 2003).

Therefore, it is of great importance to be aware of different cultural perceptions and functions of smiling. At the same time, one should not jump to conclusions about a culture's attitude towards smiling, and remember that personality, circumstances and intercultural competence also play a significant role in communication.

5. Power relations and gender

Keeping in mind that the root of smiling in primate species either reduces stress, builds relationships or, deriving from a "fear grimace", signals inferiority or (formal) subordination of the sender (Preuschoft and van Hooff, 1997, p.176, p.184), it is not surprising that low-power humans also smile more than high-power ones (LaFrance and Hecht, 1999, p.47). Low-power people feel more social pressure to smile and consequently perform more non-Duchenne smiles than their high-power partner (Ibid., p.50, p.55). In contrast, the smile of a superior sender has often a reassuring function (Preuschoft and van Hooff, 1997, p.176) or simply displays of a positive emotion, hence high-power people experience less social pressure and therefore tend to express feelings more openly (LaFrance and Hecht, 1999, p.60). These statements were confirmed in an experiment conducted by LaFrance and Hecht. Additionally, they found out that equal-power pairs smiled on average more than mixed pairs (1999, p.56).

There are significant parallels to high and low-power relations in the communication between men and women.[2] In 1970 Jakobsen differentiated the "exchange of mates" from the "exchange of women" and claimed that "expressions of status [...] and the male/female differences are the most important features [...] of human interaction." (as cited in Ritchie Key, 1980, 6f.) Women in "WEIRD"-cultures smile more than men regardless of their power status because they are expected to be more expressive, although both sexes feel emotions equally (LaFrance and Hecht, 1999, p.51). According to Henley and LaFrance smiling is not a sign of female submissiveness but rather an expression of a culture's positive values, for women are "immigrants" in a patriarchal society to which they need to adapt (1984, p.367f.). Consequently, not heightened emotions but social and cultural norms lead to the fact that women smile more (Ibid., p.353f.). The misperception of women has resulted in the presentation of smiling, 'submissive' images of women in advertisements (Rehman, 2016). These have recently been challenged in a campaign which promoted confident, serious and powerful business women. Nevertheless, the author claims that it took much effort to teach the models not to smile (Ibid.), which underlines Henley's and LaFrance's studies.

---

[2] Unfortunately, most research has been limited to Western countries.

6. Lying

It is easier to lie verbally than non-verbally hence uncontainable (micro)gestures reveal the lie visibly (Ritchie Key, 1980, p.9; Pease, 1986, p.18). When it comes to children, they do not only smile more often than adults, about twenty times more (Gutman, 2011), they also lie regularly (Lee, 2016). Against the widespread belief that a child's dishonesty is easily detected by hand-to-face gestures (Pease, 1986, p.16), children are in fact sophisticated liars and capable of maintaining a neutral expression when lying (Lee, 2016). With the help of "Transdermal Optical Imaging", which detects the change of blood flow in the face, it is possible to tell if someone is lying, hence e.g. more blood is pumped into the nose while telling a lie (Ibid.). This "Pinocchio-effect" might feel tickling and thus triggers the urge of to touch one's nose (Ibid.; Pease, 1986, p.50).

When the urge of performing a hand-to-face gesture is suppressed, smiles are sometimes used to cover a lie and thus to allay the receiver (Preuschoft 175; Pease, 1986, p.18). Consequently, smiles can be displayed voluntarily (Ekman and Keltner, 1997, p.30, p.34).

In order to detect whether a person's smile is faked, Ekman developed the "Facial Action Coding System" (FACS) which allows coders to 'read' over 40 facial expressions and differentiate Duchenne from Non-Duchenne Smiles (Ibid., p.42; Harrison, 1984, p.325). Another, more sophisticated method, is to apply electromyography (EMG) in which electrodes are used to measure facial muscle-movements that are barely visible to the naked eye (Ibid.).

Based on Ekman's achievements, the US-American TV series *Lie to Me* (2009-2011) was produced. Throughout the series, FACS and EMG are used by the *Lightman-Group* to detect whether a person speaks the truth in order to advance investigations. Although the series offers an insight into the richness of facial expressions, it does not take cultural differences into account.

7. Conclusion

The smile in intercultural communication can be compared to a chess game, in which every culture and each individual has unique rules (Ritchie Key, 1980, p.3). Therefore, a person's mindset is not as easily understood as Klineberg's statement suggested in the beginning of the paper. Based on the preceding analysis, it becomes obvious that the meaning and occasion of a person's smile are culturally and socially dependent. Particularly, the vast gap between "WEIRD" and "Non-WEIRD" societies needs to be considered. It is advisable to keep power relations and gender differences in mind, although further research concerning intercultural variety is yet to be made in these fields. Mindful communication thus goes beyond common presuppositions and requires the ability of "hearing what isn't said" (Drucker as cited in Bernstein, 2017). In the case of smiling this means that the awareness of cultural differences in the function and perception of a smile is a key element of successful non-verbal communication.

References

Bernstein, R. (2017). "Seven Cultural Differences in Nonverbal Communication". *Point Park University Online*. Retrieved April 8, 2018 from https://online.pointpark.edu/business/cultural-differences-in-nonverbal-communication/.

Condon, W. (1980). "The Relation of International Synchrony to Cognitive and Emotional Prcesses" in: *The Relationship of Verbal and Nonverbal Communication*. Ed. Ritchie Key, M. The Hague: Mouton Publishers, pp. 49-66.

Diehl, S. et al. (2003). "Advertising Effectiveness in Different Cultures: Results of an Experiment Analyzing the Effects of Individualistic and Collectivistic Advertising on Germans and Chinese." *Association for Consumer Research*. Retrieved April 8, 2018 from http://www.acrwebsite.org/search/view-conference-proceedings.aspx?Id=11732.

Ekman, P. & Keltner, D. (1997). „Universal Facial Expressions of Emotion: An Old Controversy and New Findings" in: *Nonverbal Communication: Where Nature Meets Culture*. Ed. Segerstrale, U. & Molnár, P. Mahwah: Lawrence Erlbaum Associates, pp. 27-46.

Goldhill, O. (2016). "World Leaders Smile Differently, Depending on Their Country's Culture". *Quartz*. Retrieved April 8, 2018 from https://qz.com/621624/world-leaders-smile-differently-depending-on-their-countrys-culture/.

Goldschmidt, W. (1997). "Nonverbal Communication and Culture" in: *Nonverbal Communication: Where Nature Meets Culture*. Ed. Segerstrale, U. & Molnár, P. Mahwah: Lawrence Erlbaum Associates, pp. 229-244.

Gutman, R. (2011). "The Hidden Power of Smiling". *TEDx*. Retrieved April 20, 2018 from https://www.ted.com/talks/ron_gutman_the_hidden_power_of_smiling#t-419845.

Harrison, H. (1984). "Past Problems and Future Directions in Nonverbal Behavior Research: The Case of the Face" in: *Nonverbal Behavior: Perspectives, Applications, Intercultural Insights*. Ed. Wolfgang, A. Toronto: C.J. Hogrefe, pp. 317-334.

Henley, N. & LaFrance, M. (1984). "Gender as Culture: Difference and Dominance in Non-verbal Behavior" in: *Nonverbal Behavior: Perspectives, Applications, Intercultural Insights*. Ed. Wolfgang, A. Toronto: C.J. Hogrefe, pp. 351-372.

Kendon, A. (1980). "Gesticulation and Speech: Two Aspects of the Process of Utterance" in: *The Relationship of Verbal and Nonverbal Communication*. Ed. Ritchie Key, M. The Hague: Mouton Publishers, pp. 207-228.

Khazan, O. (2016). "Why Some Cultures Frown on Smiling". *TheAtlantic*. Retrieved April 8, 2018 from https://www.theatlantic.com/science/archive/2016/05/culture-and-smiling/483827/.

Krys, K. et al (2016). "Be Careful When You Smile: Culture Shapes Judgments of Intelligence and Honesty of Smiling Individuals". *Journal of Nonverbal Behavior*, Volume 40, Issue 2, pp

101–116. *SpringerLink*. Retrieved April 8, 2018 from https://link.springer.com/article/10.1007/s10919-015-0226-4.

LaFrance, M. & Hecht, M. (1999). "Option or Obligation to Smile: The Effects of Power and Gender on Facial Expression" in: *The Social Context of Nonverbal Behavior*. Ed. Philippot, P. et al. Cambridge: Cambridge University Press, pp. 45-71.

Lee, K. (2016). "Can You Tell if a Kid is Lying?" *TEDx*. Retrieved April 20, 2018 from https://www.ted.com/talks/kang_lee_can_you_really_tell_if_a_kid_is_lying#t-799038.

Lee, V. & Wagner, H. (1999). "Facial Behavior Alone and in the Presence of Others" in: *The Social Context of Nonverbal Behavior*. Ed. Philippot, P. et al. Cambridge: Cambridge University Press, pp. 262-286.

"Lie to Me: The Science Behind the Show". *Paul Ekman Group*. Retrieved April 20, 2018 from https://www.paulekman.com/lie-to-me/.

Papousek, H. & Papousek, M. (1997). "Preverbal Communication in Humans and the Genesis of Culture" in: *Nonverbal Communication: Where Nature Meets Culture*. Ed. Segerstrale, U. & Molnár, P. Mahwah: Lawrence Erlbaum Associates, pp. 87-108.

Pease, A. (1986). *Body Language: How to Read Other's Thoughts by Their Gestures*. London: Sheldon Press.

Petersen, N. (2016). "Smiling Means Different Things in Different Cultures". *AllPsych*. Retrieved April 8, 2018 from https://www.theatlantic.com/science/archive/2016/05/culture-and-smiling/483827/ .

Pogosyan, M. (2017). "Non-verbal Communication Across Cultures". Retrieved from *PsychologyToday*. Retrieved April 8, 2018 from https://www.psychologytoday.com/us/blog/between-cultures/201706/non-verbal-communication-across-cultures.

Preuschoft, S. & van Hooff, J. (1997). "The Social Function of 'Smile' and 'Laughter': Variations Across Primate Species and Societies" in: *Nonverbal Communication: Where Nature Meets Culture*. Ed. Segerstrale, U. & Molnár, P. Mahwah: Lawrence Erlbaum Associates, pp. 171-190.

Ramsey, S. (1984). "Double Vision: Nonverbal Behavior East and West" in: *Nonverbal Behavior: Perspectives, Applications, Intercultural Insights*. Ed. Wolfgang, A. Toronto: C.J. Hogrefe, pp. 139-168.

Rehman, H. (2016). "Women, Advertising and the Power of Positive Body Language". *Huffington Post*. Retrieved April 8, 2018 from https://www.huffingtonpost.co.uk/heidy-rehman/women-advertising-the-pow_b_12954258.html.

Ritchie Key, M. (1980). "Language and Nonverbal Behavior as Organizers of Social Systems" in: *The Relationship of Verbal and Nonverbal Communication*. Ed. Ritchie Key, M. The Hague: Mouton Publishers, pp. 3-36.

Segerstrale, U. & Molnár, P. (1997). "Nonverbal Communication: Crossing the Boundary Between Culture and Nature" in: *Nonverbal Communication: Where Nature Meets Culture*. Ed. Segerstrale, U. & Molnár, P. Mahwah: Lawrence Erlbaum Associates, pp. 1-26.

"Smile". *The Oxford Dictionary*. Retrieved April 5, 2018 from https://en.oxforddictionaries.com/definition/smile.

"Ten Ways Body Language is Used in Advertising". (N.N. 2012) *Science of People*. Retrieved April 8, 2018 from https://www.scienceofpeople.com/body-language-advertising/.

"The Meaning of a Smile in Different Cultures". (N.N. 2015) *TranslateMedia*. Retrieved April 8, 2018 from https://www.translatemedia.com/us/blog-us/the-meaning-of-a-smile-in-different-cultures/.

Turner, J. (1997). "The Evolution of Emotions: The Nonverbal Basis of Human Social Organization" in: *Nonverbal Communication: Where Nature Meets Culture*. Ed. Segerstrale, U. & Molnár, P. Mahwah: Lawrence Erlbaum Associates, pp. 211-228.

Weiberg, P. & Konert, F.J. (1984). "Emotional Facial Expressions in Advertising" *Advances in Consumer Research*, Volume 11, pp 607-611. *Association for Consumer Research*. Retrieved April 8, 2018 from http://acrwebsite.org/volumes/6316/volumes/v11/NA-11.